© for the Spanish original edition: 2019, Mosquito Books, Barcelona
www.mosquitobooksbarcelona.com
© for the English edition: 2019, Prestel Verlag, Munich · London · New York
A member of Verlagsgruppe Random House GmbH
Neumarkter Strasse 28 · 81673 Munich
© for the illustrations: 2019, María Suárez Inclán
© for the text: 2019, Mia Cassany

Prestel Publishing Ltd.
14-17 Wells Street
London W1T 3PD

Prestel Publishing
900 Broadway, Suite 603
New York, NY 10003

Library of Congress Control Number: 2018965318
A CIP catalogue record for this book is available from the British Library.

Translated from the Spanish by Daniel Kaasikas
Copyediting: Brad Finger
Project management: Melanie Schöni
Production management: Susanne Hermann
Typesetting: Susanne Hermann and Carolin Michnick
Printing and binding: DZS Grafik, Slovenia
Paper: Tauro Offset

Verlagsgruppe Random House FSC® N001967

Printed in Slovenia

ISBN 978-3-7913-7404-8
www.prestel.com

THE BIG BOOK OF EVERYTHING YOU NEED TO GET THE JOB DONE

PRESTEL

Munich · London · New York

MUSICIAN

Vinyl record

Cassette player

Trumpet

Maracas

Microphone

Music stand

Which of these instruments do you play by blowing into them?

Triangle

Harmonica

Tambourine

Bow

Electronic keyboard

Flute

Djembe or African drum

Guitar case

Microphone

Cymbals

Harp

Cassette tape

Xylophone

Electric piano

Drumsticks

player

Cello

Drum

ic guitar

Grand piano

French horn

Sheet music

Conga drums

ead-
ones

Baton

Musical instruments
can be winds, strings
or percussion. They can
even be electronic. Also,
some of the objects shown
here are useful for listening
to music, while others
can accompany you
when you sing.
Let's play!

ARTIST

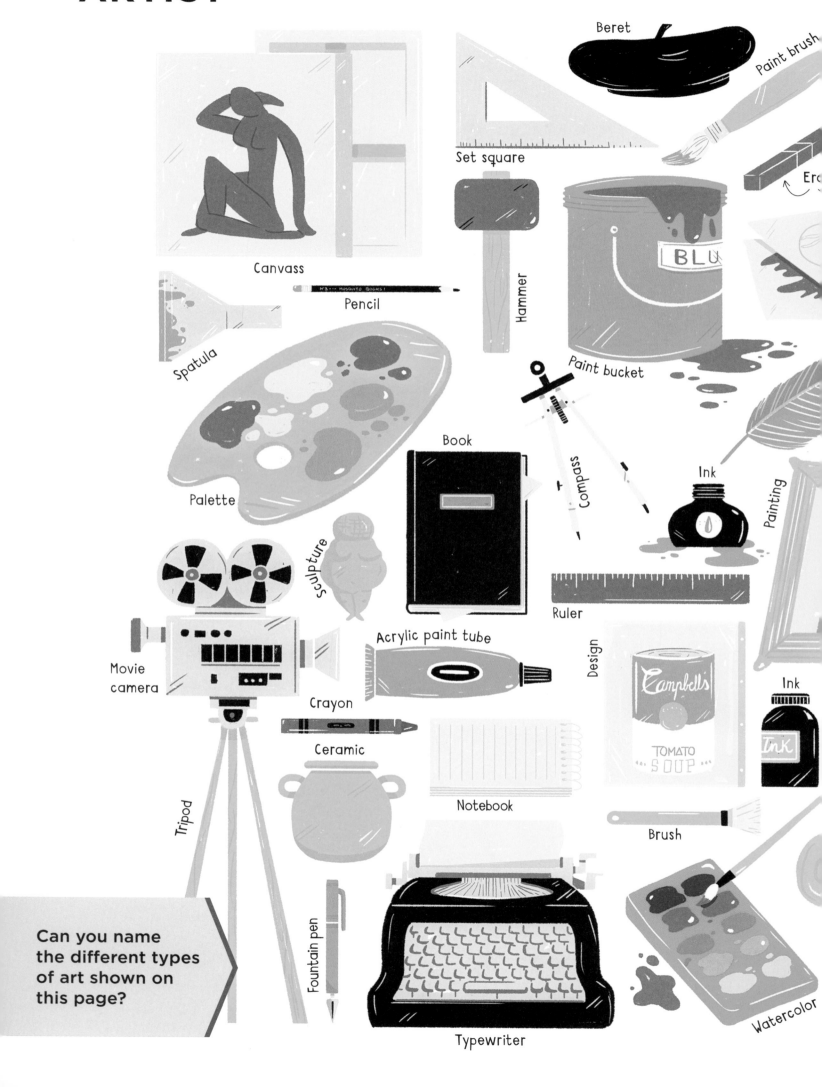

Beret

Paint brush

Set square

Hammer

Canvass

Pencil

Spatula

Palette

BLU

Paint bucket

Compass

Book

Ink

Painting

Sculpture

Ruler

Movie camera

Acrylic paint tube

Design

Crayon

Ink

Ceramic

Notebook

Tripod

Brush

Fountain pen

Typewriter

Watercolor

Can you name the different types of art shown on this page?

Paint brush

Scale

Protractor

Everyone who makes art has a unique, creative mind. All of us are capable of taking our own ideas and transforming them into a beautiful picture, a funny movie, an exciting story or an impressive sculpture.

Drawing

Awl

Artwork

Fan brush

Antiquity

Quill

Paint tubes

Eraser

Easel

Folding ruler

Film reel

Pencil sharpener

Set square

Pencil

Camera

t can

Roller

Column

Box cutter

Flash

Bust

Spatula

Roll of film

FILM

NATURE EXPLORER

Fingerprint book

Match

Bug

Magnifying glass

Binoculars

Thread

Camping tent

Badge

Ax

Swiss Army knife

Badge

Cap

Flashlight

Branch

Radio

Map

How many badges can you see?

Slingshot

Fire

Fishing rod

Baseball cap

Oars

First aid kit

Apple

Badges

Badge

Explorer's hat

Mushroom

Arrow

Bow

ms

et

Notebook

Compass

Backpack

Butterflies

Acorn

Cup

Flag

Camera

Water bottle

Butterfly net

Leaf

Leaf

Canoe

Lamp

Many people around the world work in natural environments. Explorers travel to new places, biologists study wild animals and their behavior, and foresters help make sure people don't litter or cause harmful fires in the forest.

DOCTOR

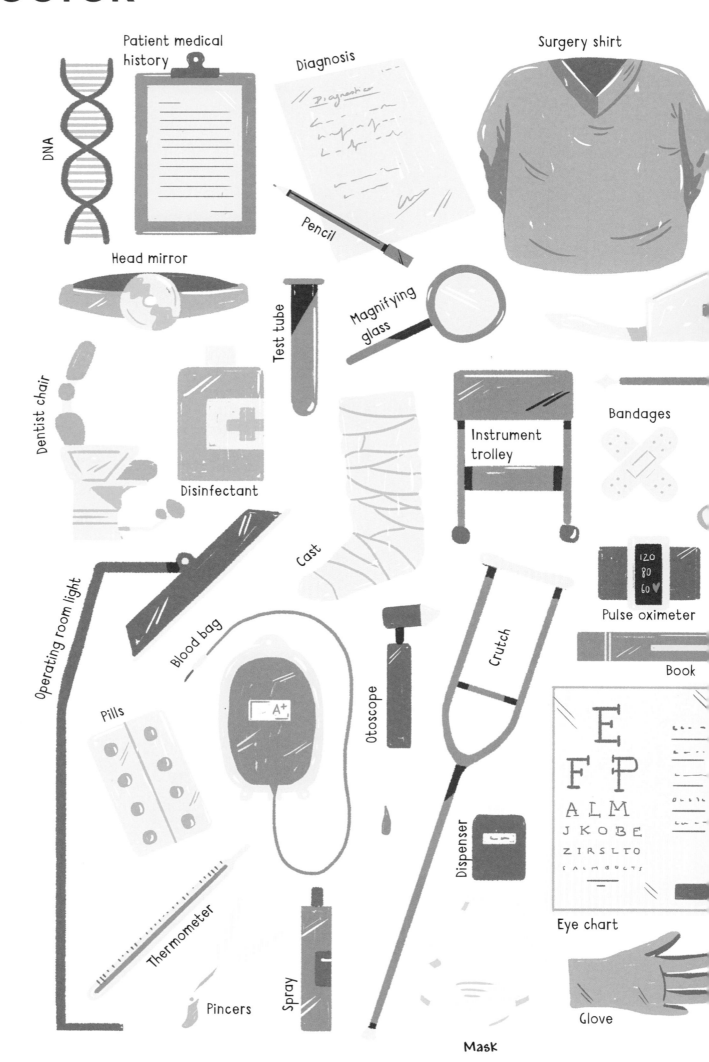

DNA

Patient medical history

Diagnosis

Surgery shirt

Pencil

Head mirror

Test tube

Magnifying glass

Dentist chair

Disinfectant

Instrument trolley

Bandages

Cast

Operating room light

Blood bag

Otoscope

Crutch

Pulse oximeter

Book

Pills

A⁺

Eye chart

Dispenser

E
F P
A L M
J K O B E
Z I R S L T O

Thermometer

Spray

Pincers

Glove

Mask

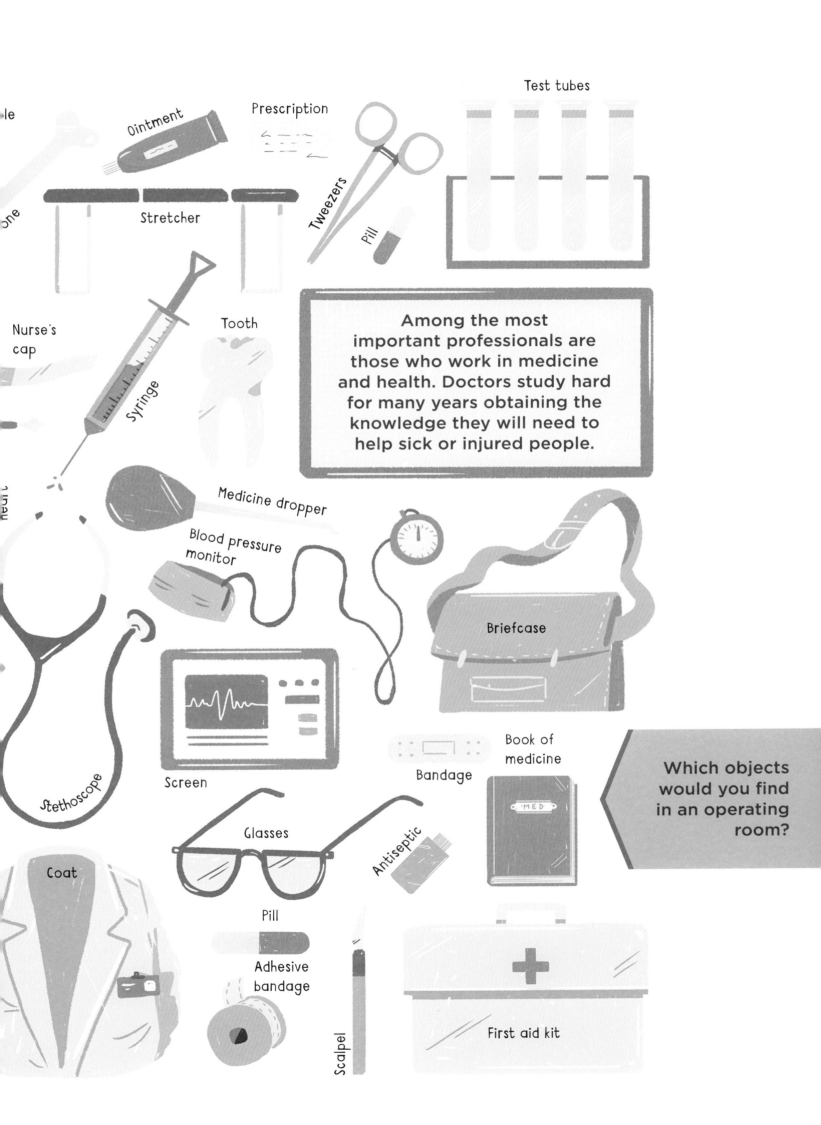

Ointment

Prescription

Test tubes

...le

...one

Stretcher

Tweezers

Pill

Nurse's cap

Tooth

Syringe

Among the most important professionals are those who work in medicine and health. Doctors study hard for many years obtaining the knowledge they will need to help sick or injured people.

Medicine dropper

Blood pressure monitor

Briefcase

Stethoscope

Screen

Bandage

Book of medicine

MED

Which objects would you find in an operating room?

Coat

Glasses

Antiseptic

Pill

Adhesive bandage

Scalpel

First aid kit

MECHANIC

Hard hat

Hammer

Work shirt

Screwdriver

Hammer

Screw

Wrench

Cog

Cable cutters

Wheel

Adjustable

Boots

Welding

Book

Notebook

Fuel can

Ladder

Hacksaw

Ruler

Air pump

Tool box

Measuring tape

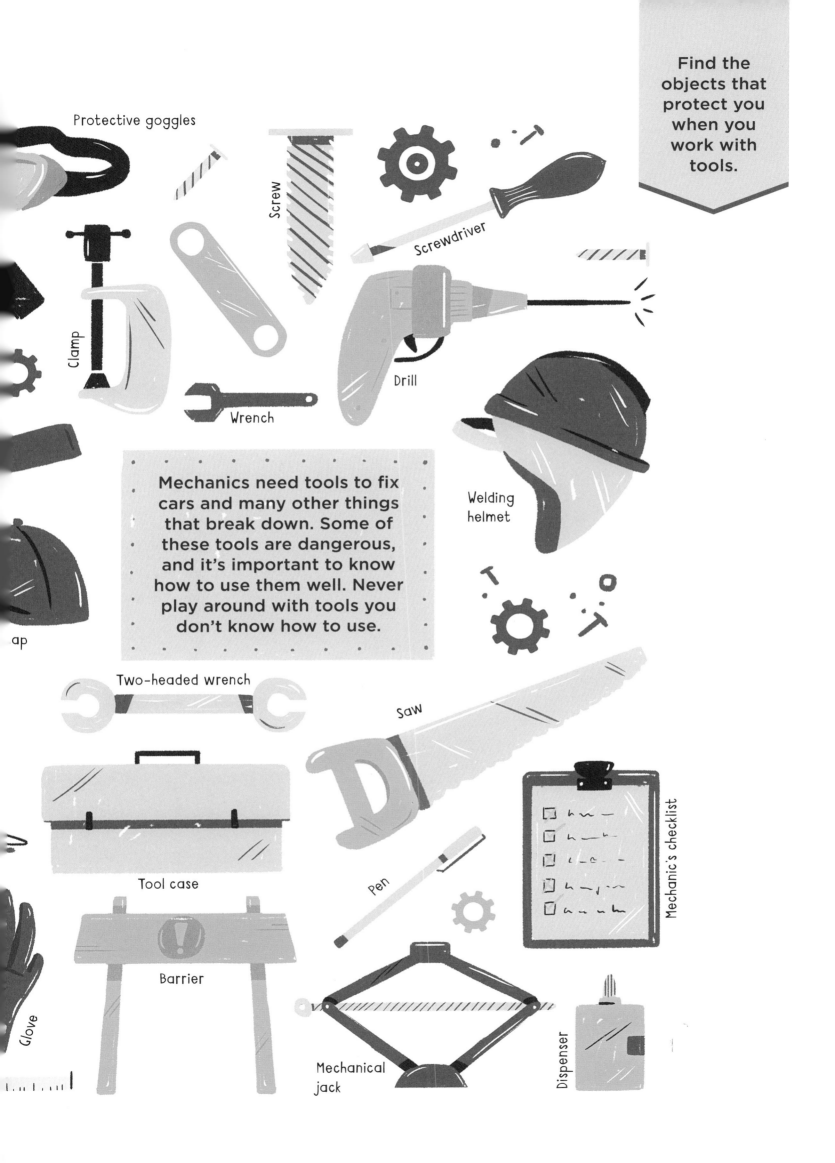

Find the objects that protect you when you work with tools.

Protective goggles

Screw

Screwdriver

Clamp

Drill

Wrench

Welding helmet

Mechanics need tools to fix cars and many other things that break down. Some of these tools are dangerous, and it's important to know how to use them well. Never play around with tools you don't know how to use.

ap

Two-headed wrench

Saw

Tool case

Pen

Mechanic's checklist

Barrier

Glove

Mechanical jack

Dispenser

CHEF

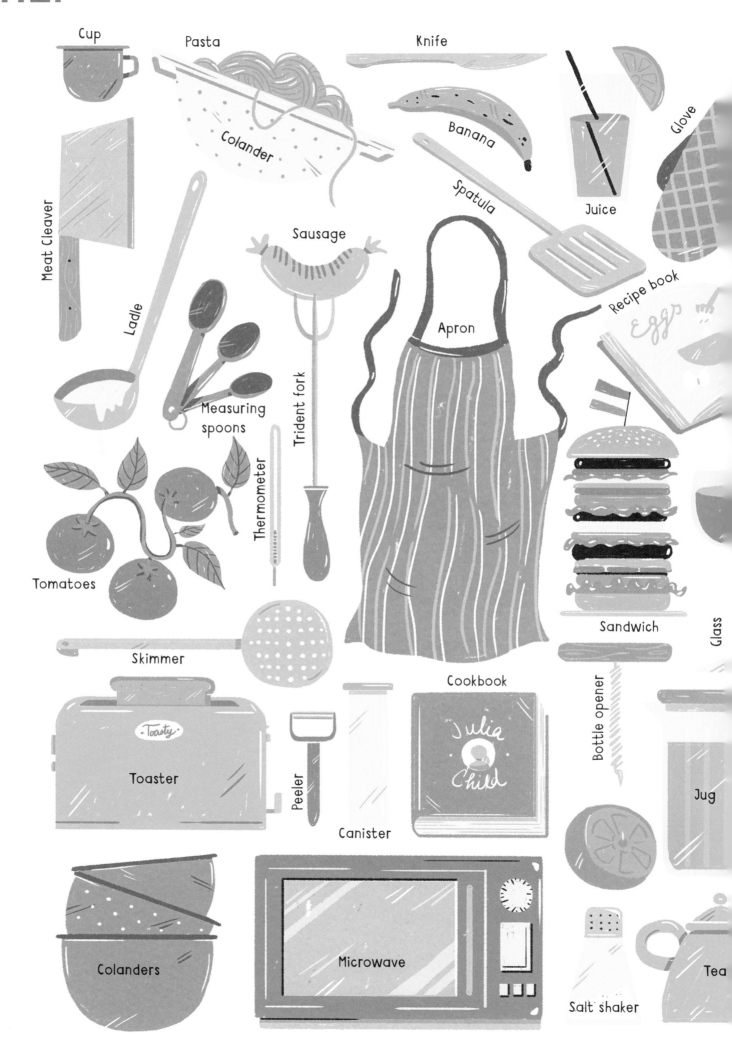

Cup

Pasta

Colander

Knife

Banana

Spatula

Glove

Juice

Meat Cleaver

Sausage

Apron

Recipe book

eggs

Ladle

Measuring spoons

Trident fork

Thermometer

Tomatoes

Sandwich

Glass

Skimmer

Cookbook

Bottle opener

Toaster

Peeler

Julia Child

Jug

Canister

Colanders

Microwave

Tea

Salt shaker

Roller

Tea filter

Fried egg

Sausages

Working in a kitchen is an important job. Chefs can make dishes by using old recipes and traditions from the past. They can also use their imagination, intuition and originality to create new and delicious flavors.

Salt mill

Cooking pot

Pan

Name the objects here that can help you measure a cooking ingredient.

Cheese grater

Whisk

awberry

Cheese

Saucepan

Chef's hat

Timer

Sausage

Bottle

Fork

Oven mitt

Apple

Scale

Measuring cup

Cup

Coffee maker

Scraper spatula

MILK

Milk carton

GARDENER

Shovel

Plant

Watering can

Hat

Trowel

Rake

Ax

Soil

Basket

Cac[tus]

Tractor

Saw

Shears

Hose

Dripper

Fertilizer

Sack

Plant label

Planter

Which of these objects are used for watering?

Pincers

Bucket

Seeds

Spade

Leaf

Boot

Watering can

Tomato plant

Sprayer

Carrot

Pot

Plant pot

Gardening used to be done far away from the big cities. Today, however, more and more city people can work on rooftop gardens, green spaces in their neighborhoods, or micro-gardens in their own homes.

Sprayer

Scythe

Fertilizer

Gloves

Wheelbarrow

Shoots

Pitchfork

ATHLETE

Cap

Chronometer

Racket

Whistle

Basketball hoo[p]

Baseball

Ball

Bowling ball

Badminton racket

Baseball bat

Bowling pins

Medal

Football

Football boot

Target board

American football helmet

Flag

Hockey stick

Ski pole

Gym rope

Pole

Pool ball

Ice skate

Bag

Riding helmet

Swimming goggles

Water polo ball

Which of these objects are not used by athletes when playing sports? Who uses them?

Hiking sock

Weights

Golf ball

Trophy

American football

Tennis shoe

Golf club

Table tennis racket

Baseball jersey

fboard

Badminton shuttlecock

oxing ove

Arrow

Weights

Visor

All professional athletes need discipline and perseverance to succeed. Training is necessary to improve a little bit each day. Athletes should also realize that they cannot win every time they play.

Sports bag

COMPUTER SCIENTIST

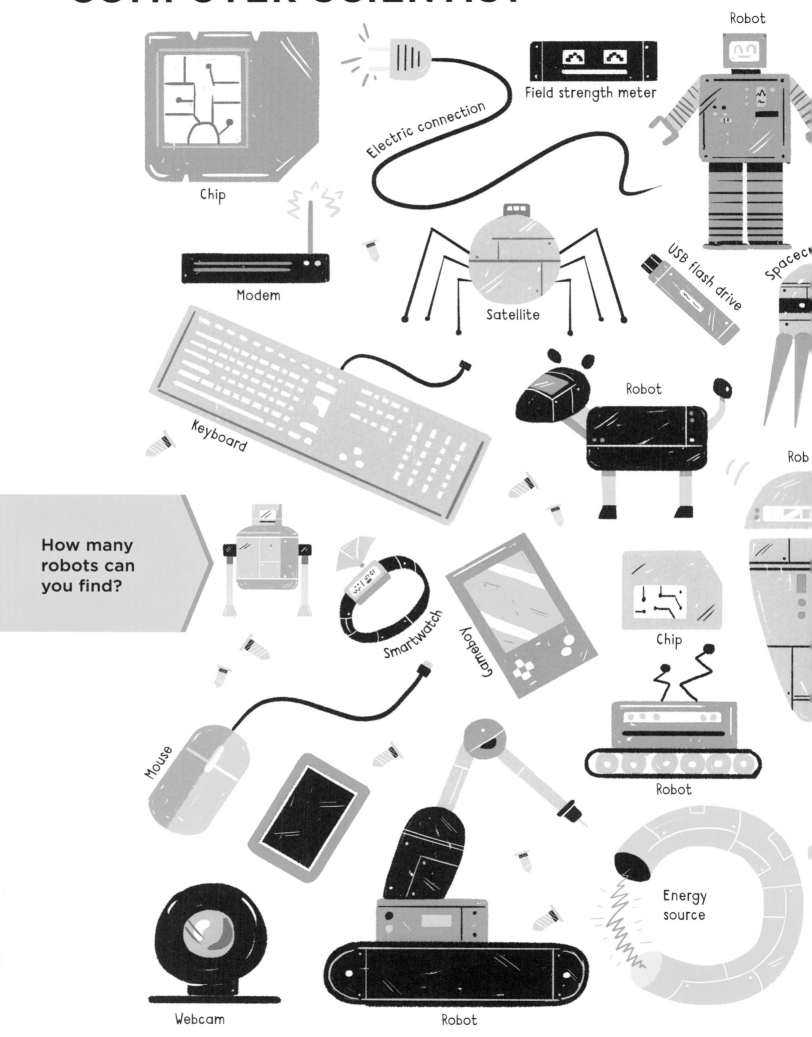

Chip

Electric connection

Field strength meter

Robot

Modem

Satellite

USB flash drive

Spacec

Keyboard

Robot

Rob

How many robots can you find?

Smartwatch

Gameboy

Chip

Mouse

Chip

Robot

Webcam

Robot

Energy source

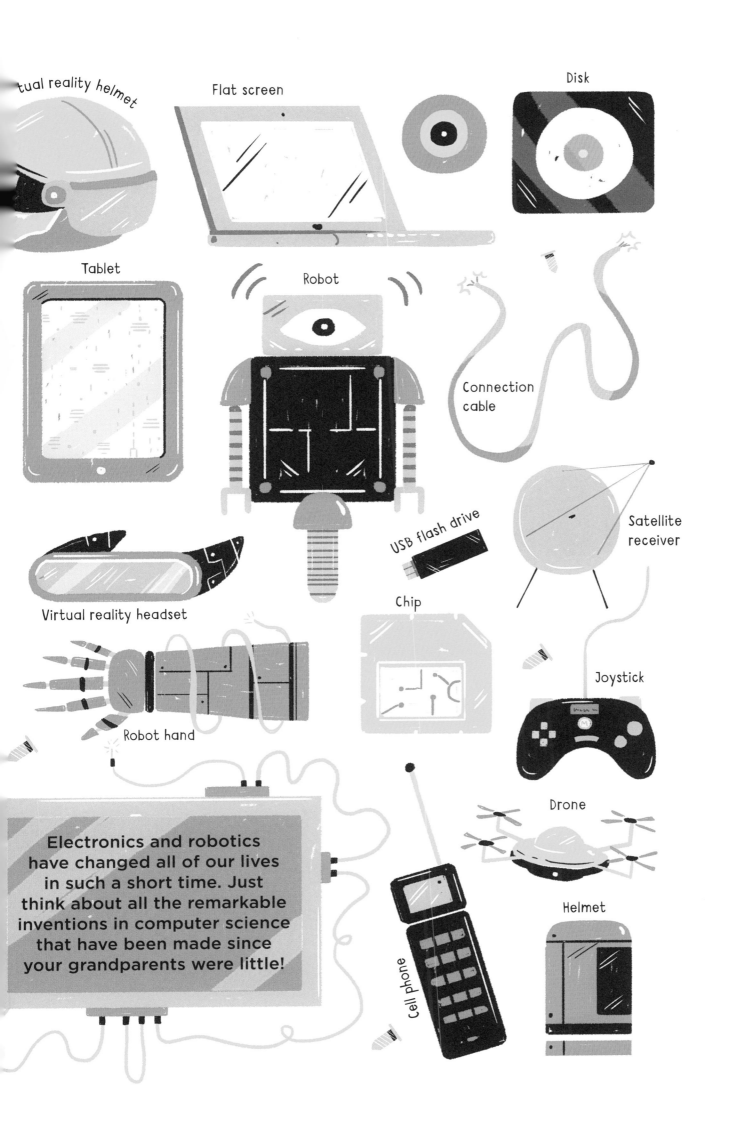

tual reality helmet

Flat screen

Disk

Tablet

Robot

Connection cable

Virtual reality headset

USB flash drive

Satellite receiver

Robot hand

Chip

Joystick

Drone

Electronics and robotics have changed all of our lives in such a short time. Just think about all the remarkable inventions in computer science that have been made since your grandparents were little!

Cell phone

Helmet

Find three objects that do not belong to the profession of these characters.

(*) THE CHEF does not need: the cassette tape, the brush or the cactus.
THE GARDENER does not need: the swimming goggles, the toaster or the gameboy.

Find three objects that
do not belong to the profession
of these characters.

(*) THE MUSICIAN does not need: the heart, the perfume or the watering can.
THE ATHLETE does not need: the duckling, the screws or the scissors.

Find three objects that do not belong to the profession of these characters.

Find three objects that
do not belong to the profession
of these characters.

(*) THE ARTIST does not need: the robot, the ax or the compass.
THE NATURE EXPLORER does not need: the stethoscope, the badminton shuttlecock or the modem.

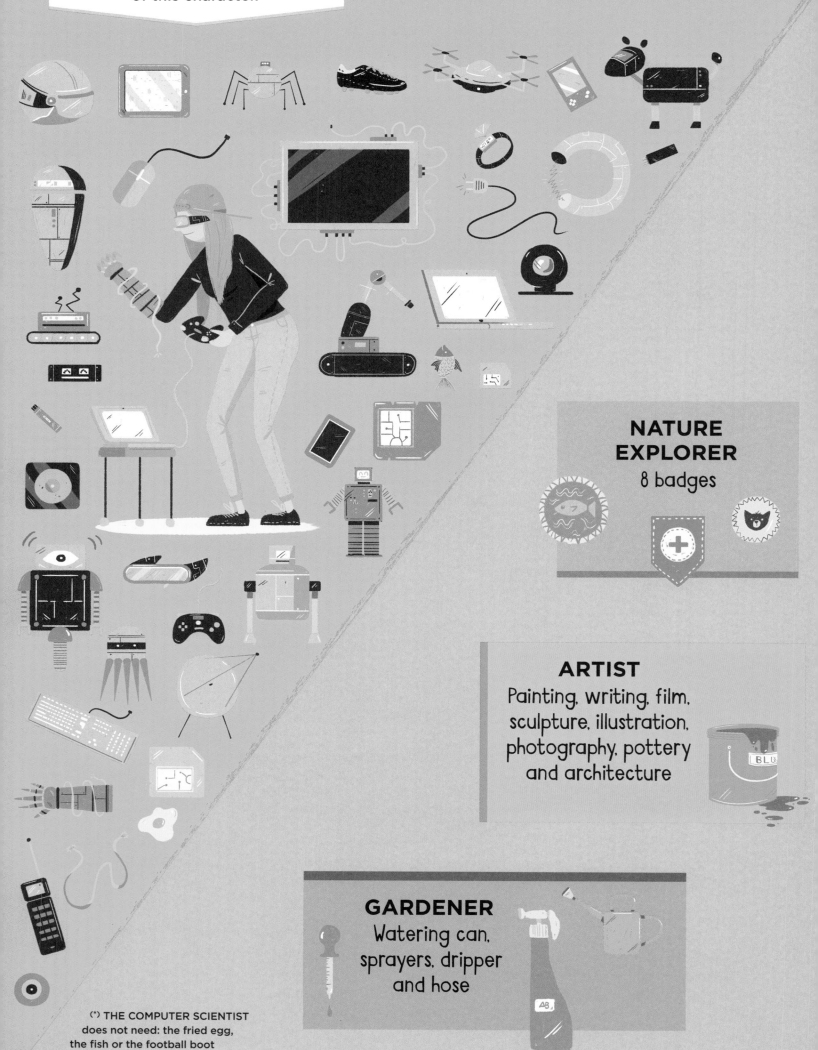

Find three objects that do not belong to the profession of this character.

(*) THE COMPUTER SCIENTIST does not need: the fried egg, the fish or the football boot

SOLUTIONS

COMPUTER SCIENTIST
6 robots

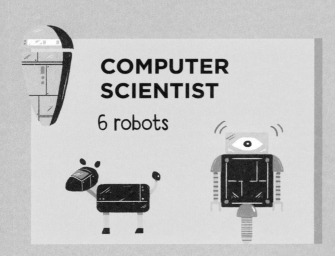

MUSICIAN
Trumpet, French horn, flute, harmonica

MECHANIC
Goggles, helmets, boots and gloves

DOCTOR
Surgery shirt, pincers, tweezers, scalpels, instrument trolley, screen, operating room light, mask, gloves

CHEF
The scale, the measuring spoons and the measuring cup

ATHLETE
The chronometer and the whistle are used by the referee.

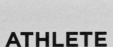

When you grow up, what job would you like to do?